THE LIBRARY OF
CONSTELLATIONS™

Gemini

Stephanie True Peters

The Rosen Publishing Group's
PowerKids Press™
New York

For Tavo and Tamsin, my favorite twins

Published in 2003 by The Rosen Publishing Group, Inc.
29 East 21st Street, New York, NY 10010

First Edition

Editor: Natashya Wilson
Book Design: Michael J. Caroleo, Michael Donnellan, Michael de Guzman

Photo Credits: Cover, p. 4 © Roger Ressmeyer/CORBIS; back cover, title page, p. 8 Bode's Uranographia, 1801, courtesy of the Science, Industry & Business Library, the New York Public Library, Astor, Lenox and Tilden Foundations; pp. 6, 7, 12 © Stapleton Collection/CORBIS; p. 11 © NASA; p. 15 (top left) © PhotoDisc, (bottom right) © Bettmann/CORBIS; p. 16 © John Foster/Photo Researchers, graphic enhancement by Michael Donnellan; p. 19 © Jonathan Blair/CORBIS; p. 20 NOAO/AURA/NSF.

Peters, Stephanie True, 1965–
Gemini / Stephanie True Peters.— 1st ed.
p. cm. — (The library of constellations)
Includes bibliographical references and index.
Summary: Provides historic and scientific information about the constellation Gemini as well as about stars in general.
  ISBN 0-8239-6167-2 (library binding)
1. Gemini (Constellation)—Juvenile literature. 2. Zodiac—Juvenile literature. [1. Gemini (Constellation) 2. Zodiac. 3. Constellations. 4. Stars.]
I. Title. II. Series: Peters, Stephanie True, 1965–.
Library of constellations.
  QB803 .P42 2003
  523.8—dc21

2001004549

Manufactured in the United States of America

Contents

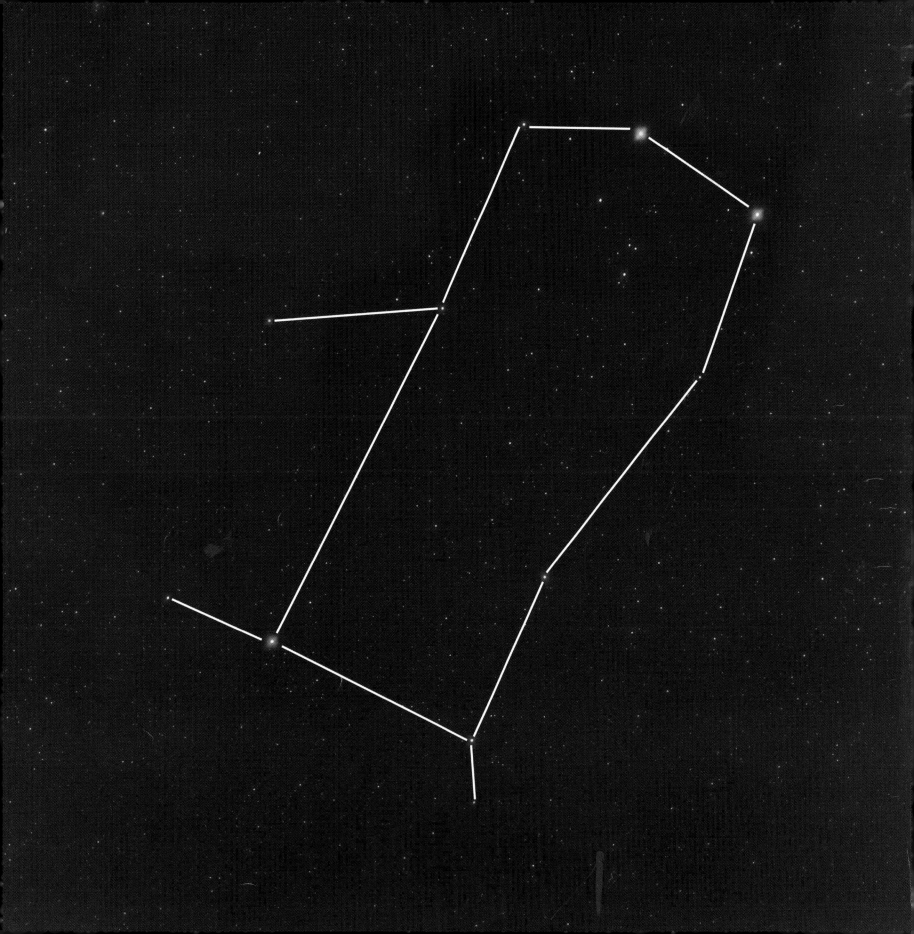

The Twins

For centuries people have looked at the sky at night and have imagined that they saw people and other things outlined in the stars. The group of stars that makes up an outline is called a constellation. The constellation named Gemini, also known as the Twins, is thought to look like twin brothers.

Gemini is shaped like a crooked rectangle. The two brightest stars in the constellation mark the rectangle's top corners. These stars are named Castor and Pollux. They represent the Twins' heads. Two crooked lines of stars make up the rectangle's sides. These sides form the Twins' bodies. Two dim stars sit just outside of the rectangle's bottom corners, one on each side. They complete the Twins' legs. Other stars outside of the rectangle form the Twins' arms. People have imagined that the Twins are walking, arm in arm.

In this outline of Gemini, Pollux is the bright star at the top of the rectangle's left side. Castor is the bright star at the top of the rectangle's right side.

5

How to Find the Twins

Gemini can be found in the night sky of the Northern **Hemisphere** from November to April. In the Southern Hemisphere, Gemini can be found in the night sky from December to March. The easiest way to locate Gemini is to find the constellation **Orion**, the Hunter. Orion is a large constellation marked by a line of three stars that represents Orion's belt. Above and to the left of the belt is **Betelgeuse**, a very bright star that marks Orion's shoulder. This star points the way above Orion to the Twins. Once you look above Orion, the stars Castor and Pollux will be easy to see, because they are bright and close to each other.

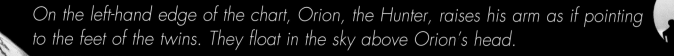

On the left-hand edge of the chart, Orion, the Hunter, raises his arm as if pointing to the feet of the twins. They float in the sky above Orion's head.

The Gemini Myth

There is a Greek myth, or very old story, that tells how twin brothers came to be in the sky. Gemini's brightest stars are named for these twins, Castor and Pollux. The twins' mother was Leda, the queen of Sparta. The twins were said to have different fathers, even though the babies were born at the same time. Castor's father was Tyndareus, the king of Sparta. Pollux's father was Zeus, the king of the Greek gods. Castor was mortal, like his father, Tyndareus. Pollux was immortal, like his father, Zeus. They were together all the time as they grew up. Castor became a horseman and a soldier. Pollux became a boxer. When Castor was killed by an angry cattleman, Pollux begged Zeus to kill him, too. Instead Zeus brought Castor back to life every other day. On the days that Castor was not alive, Pollux was allowed to visit him in the world of the dead. Later Zeus placed the twins side by side in the sky as the constellation Gemini.

The ancient Romans called the Twins in the sky Romulus and Remus, for the twin brothers who founded Rome in Roman myth.

9

The Eskimo Nebula

Castor and Pollux aren't the only two figures linked to Gemini. Gemini is also home to the Eskimo **Nebula**, also called the Clownface Nebula. A nebula is a cloud of space dust and gas. There are several kinds of nebulae. The Eskimo Nebula is a **planetary nebula**. It looks round, like a planet. Planetary nebulae are created when old stars die. As a star gets older, it swells in size. Eventually its outer layers are blown away, making a cloud of dust and gases. The leftover inside, or core, of the old star is so hot that it glows. The glow from the hot core lights up the cloud around the old star, creating a planetary nebula.

German astronomer William Herschel discovered the Eskimo Nebula in 1787. This bluish green nebula is located just outside the line of stars that represent Pollux's body, near the top of the rectangle. When seen through a powerful telescope, the nebula appears to have a face. The face has two dark eyes, a dark mouth, a bright nose, and a furry collar.

Ninety-five percent of all stars will eventually form planetary nebulae. The Sun will become a planetary nebula billions of years from now.

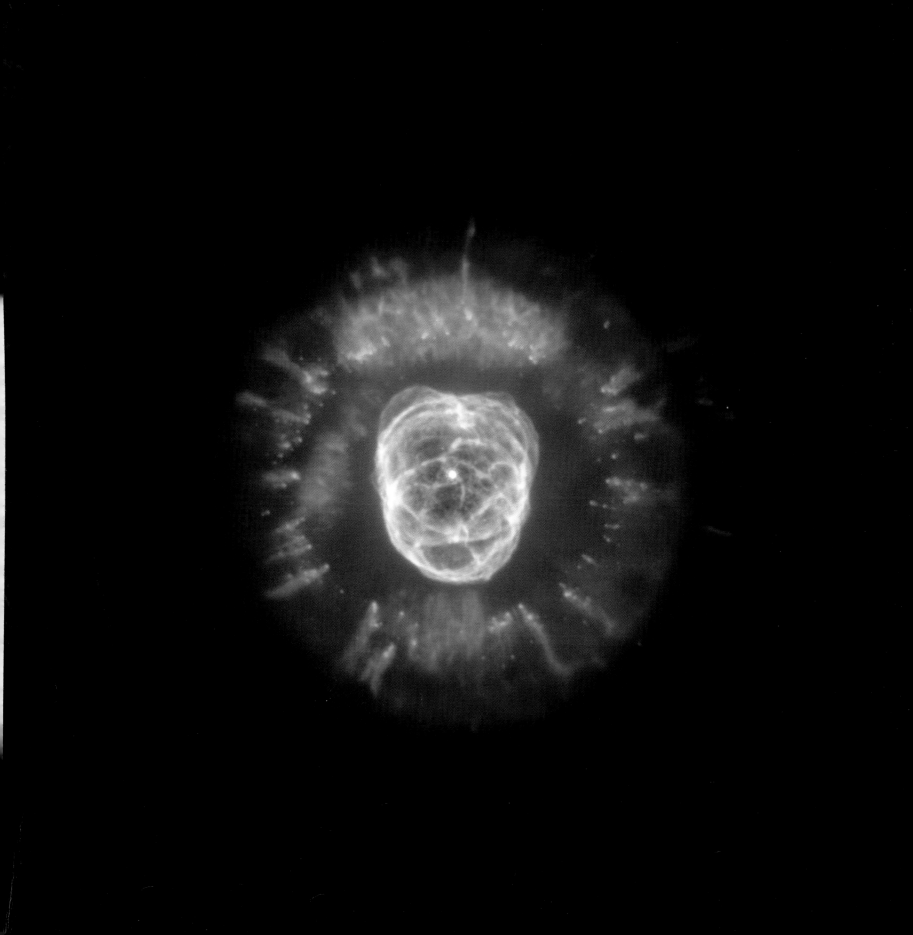

The Zodiac

Gemini is one of the 12 constellations of the **zodiac**. *Zodiac* is a Greek word that means "the circle of animals." Many of the zodiac constellations are named for animals. You cannot see all 12 zodiac constellations at once. You can see them all during the course of one year, however. They form a long line in the sky. The line of constellations seems to move around Earth, but it actually does not. Earth makes a complete circle, or **orbit**, around the Sun in one year. Earth's orbit follows the line of the zodiac constellations. As Earth moves throughout the year, different zodiac constellations come into view at night. Like Earth, the other planets in our **solar system** orbit the Sun. They also pass through the zodiac constellations. By studying the planets' movements through the zodiac, astronomers learn how planets move through space.

In ancient times people thought that the zodiac constellations circled Earth. They made charts like this one to show the zodiac's movement.

William Herschel

William Herschel was born in Germany in 1738. He moved to England in 1757, and he became interested in **astronomy**. In 1781, he began looking at Gemini through his handmade telescope. One night in March, he noticed that a bright dot he'd seen the night before had changed position. Night after night, he watched as the dot slowly moved through the constellation. At first Herschel thought he was looking at a **comet**, which is a ball of ice and space dust that orbits the Sun. Finally he and other **astronomers** realized the dot was a planet that no one had seen before. They named the planet Uranus.

Uranus is the seventh planet from the Sun in our solar system. It has 15 moons and is blue-green in color. Uranus is four times the size of Earth. It takes Uranus 84 years to orbit the Sun!

Fun Facts

Uranus orbits the Sun with its north and south poles tilted sideways to the Sun. Every so often, when a pole points toward the Sun, one day on Uranus lasts for 42 Earth years!

When William Herschel discovered Uranus, he was looking at Gemini through a telescope that he built. Herschel taught himself astronomy.

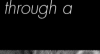

Uranus

Pollux and Castor

Pollux is the brightest star in Gemini. It is the seventeenth-brightest star that we can see in the night sky! Pollux's twin, Castor, is not as bright, but it is just as exciting. Castor is not one star, but six separate stars. A star like Castor is called a **multiple star**. Castor is made up of three pairs of **double stars**. A double star is two stars that circle around a common center. **Gravity** keeps the two stars together. Two of Castor's double stars are close together and easy to see through a telescope. The third double star is farther away from the other two and looks much fainter. When seen with the naked eye, these six stars blur together to make one bright star.

Fun Facts

A new star is made of a gas called hydrogen. Gravity in the star squeezes the hydrogen gas so much that it turns into another gas, called helium. This change in gas is what makes stars shine!

Castor and Pollux shine brightly in the sky over the Parade of Elephants rock formation in Arches National Park, Utah.

The Geminid Meteor Shower

Castor marks the spot to look for one of the night sky's sights, the Geminid **meteor** shower. A meteor is a piece of rock or space dust that burns up as it passes through Earth's **atmosphere**. As it burns, it looks like a streak of light that flashes across the night sky. Many people call meteors shooting stars or falling stars. When 20 or more meteors flash across the sky within an hour, astronomers call the event a meteor shower. In a meteor shower, a stream of dust and debris enters Earth's atmosphere and burns up. In the middle of December, there is a 10-day meteor shower called the Geminid. The meteors appear to start their trip across the sky at Castor. The meteors are called the Geminids, which means "children of Gemini." During the Geminid meteor shower, from 50 to 80 meteors appear each hour.

Scientists believe that the dinosaurs might have died after a huge meteor hit Earth about 65 million years ago. The meteor might have been 6 miles (10 km) wide at its widest point!

This picture of the Geminid meteor shower was taken from inside Meteor Crater in Arizona. The crater was formed when a meteor hit Earth about 50,000 years ago.

M35, the Open Star Cluster

Gemini is the home of M35, a beautiful **open star cluster**. An open star cluster is a small group of stars loosely held together by gravity. The M in M35 stands for Messier, the last name of astronomer Charles Messier. Messier lived from 1730 to 1817. He discovered many objects in the night sky and published a list of the objects he found. Gemini's open star cluster was the thirty-fifth object on the list, so it is named M35. The number of stars in an open star cluster varies from 10 to 1,000. M35 is made of about 200 stars. It is located just above the star that represents Castor's leg. It can be seen with **binoculars** or with a small **telescope**.

Fun Facts

The stars in open star clusters are young stars that are slowly moving away from one another. This means that the shapes of open star clusters change. A group of old stars that are bunched together is called a globular cluster. Stars in globular clusters stay together in the same shapes.

Most of the stars in the M35 open star cluster are younger than the Sun.

Other Twin Myths

Many cultures around the world imagined Gemini as twin objects. More than 3,000 years ago, the ancient Egyptians described the Twins as two plants sprouting from the earth. They also described the Twins as two goats. Hundreds of years later, the Arabs looked at the Twins and saw two peacocks. The Hindus called the Twins the **Asvins**, who were warrior-god twins on horseback. Wandering hunters who lived in the deserts of South Africa said the Twins were the two wives of an antelope god. Ancient Greeks and Romans thought the Twins were lucky for sailors. Roman sailors would call on the Twins for luck by saying, "by Gemini." Today this phrase has become "by jiminy."

Fun Facts

The stars Castor and Pollux look as if they are close to each other in the sky, but they really are not! Castor is about 52 light-years away from Earth. Pollux is about 35 light-years from Earth. A light-year is the distance light can travel in one year, about 6 trillion miles (10 trillion km).

Glossary

astronomers (uh-STRAH-nuh-merz) Scientists who study the stars and other objects in space.

astronomy (uh-STRAH-nuh-mee) The study of the stars and other objects in space.

Asvins (AS-vinz) Hindu twin warrior-gods who rode horses.

atmosphere (AT-muh-sfeer) The layer of gas that surrounds Earth.

Betelgeuse (BEE-tl-joos) A bright star found in the constellation Orion.

binoculars (bih-NAH-kyuh-lurz) Handheld lenses that, when you look through them, make objects seem closer.

comet (KAH-mit) A ball of ice and space dust that looks like a star with a tail of light.

double stars (DUH-bl STARZ) Two stars that circle around a common center.

gravity (GRA-vih-tee) The force that pulls objects toward one another.

hemisphere (HEH-muh-sfeer) Half of a round ball. The Northern Hemisphere is the northern half of Earth, and the Southern Hemisphere is the southern half.

meteor (MEE-tee-or) A speck of space dirt that burns when it enters Earth's atmosphere. A shooting star.

multiple star (MUL-tih-pl STAR) Two or more stars kept close together by gravity. They look like one star when seen with the naked eye.

nebula (NEH-byuh-luh) A cloud of dust and gas in space.

open star cluster (OH-pen STAR KLUS-ter) A group of stars held together by gravity.

orbit (OR-bit) A circular movement that one object makes around another.

Orion (oh-RY-un) The Hunter, from Greek mythology; a large constellation found in the winter sky.

planetary nebula (PLA-neh-teh-ree NEH-byuh-luh) A lit-up, round cloud of dust and gas that forms as an old star dies.

solar system (SOH-ler SIS-tem) Our Sun and the nine planets that circle around it.

telescope (TEH-leh-skohp) An instrument that uses lenses and mirrors to magnify objects in the night sky.

zodiac (ZOH-dee-ak) The 12 constellations that seem to circle Earth in a straight line.

Index

Web Sites

To learn more about constellations and Gemini, check out these Web sites:
www.astro.wisc.edu/~dolan/constellations
www.dibonsmith.com/stars.htm
   www.dustbunny.com/afk/